COMMON DISASTER

COMMON DISASTER

poems

M. CYNTHIA CHEUNG

CINCINNATI 2025

Acre Books is made possible by the support of the Robert and Adele Schiff Foundation and the Department of English at the University of Cincinnati.

Printed in the United States of America

ISBN-13 (pbk) 978-1-946724-98-4
ISBN-13 (ebook) 978-1-946724-99-1

Designed by Barbara Neely Bourgoyne
Cover art: Unsplash/愚木混株 cdd20

The press is based at the University of Cincinnati, Department of English, Arts & Sciences Hall, Room 248, PO Box 210069, Cincinnati, OH, 45221-0069.

Acre Books titles may be purchased at a discount for educational use.
For information please email business@acre-books.com.

for my family

COMMON DISASTER

poems

M. CYNTHIA CHEUNG

CINCINNATI 2025

Acre Books is made possible by the support of the Robert and Adele Schiff Foundation and the Department of English at the University of Cincinnati.

Printed in the United States of America

ISBN-13 (pbk) 978-1-946724-98-4
ISBN-13 (ebook) 978-1-946724-99-1

Designed by Barbara Neely Bourgoyne
Cover art: Unsplash/愚木混株 cdd20

The press is based at the University of Cincinnati, Department of English, Arts & Sciences Hall, Room 248, PO Box 210069, Cincinnati, OH, 45221-0069.

Acre Books titles may be purchased at a discount for educational use.
For information please email business@acre-books.com.

CONTENTS

III

COMMON DISASTER

Boreal Time

To have evolved. To survive the retreat of glaciers. To travel distances across the earth in a soft body, naked except for the tightly coiled shell—a living speck of flesh that cannot live without long-vanished Pleistocene air. To make a mollusk's last stand: wolfsbane-covered slope where a river of ice reclines under bedrock, exhales through cracked talus. Each breath, the present. More bodies gliding silently over leaf litter. To follow the deepest instinct. To converge. They cannot hear the jet trail miles above. They do not look up. Translucent eggs exquisite and hibernal, not questioning, not demanding. To exist where everything melts.

I

Ghazal

Down the hole now—we descend these caves to divert ourselves.
We return to Lascaux, to Chauvet, to find the origins of ourselves:

humans—still speechless—brushing animal-pictures into the under-
world they stumbled across, or perhaps invented themselves.

Yet the moisture of our breath corrodes, stings like night advancing
under the crush of Richter 7.8 destruction. Easier to ask ourselves

why *H. sapiens* still exists but *H. neanderthalensis* doesn't.
Across the Syrian border, the survivors exhaust themselves.

Why must they excavate children's bodies with bare fingers, red
handprints like mirrors of Altamira's? Do we inspect ourselves

with the same certainty we pretend when declaring we're different
from the rest of creation? Scientists had to see the caves themselves

before believing archaic men capable of thought, of transforming
silence—the inner world—into dark holograms of themselves.

In fact, in Altamira, our ancestors painted nothing but predator
after predator. Should we act surprised we've always been ourselves?

I Have Seen My Death

—ANNA BERTHA ROENTGEN, 1895

In physics, *x* represents the unknown.
When Anna's husband discovered a strange
new radiation, he named it and made history's
first image of a living hand: her fingers'
bones and, on the fourth digit, the ring floating,
as if around a planet.

*

When I was six, I unfolded an artist's
rendition of the solar system from the center
of an old *National Geographic* and discovered
that the sun would dilate within five billion years and overtake
the Earth. I couldn't decide which was worse—this
or extinction.

*

It's true that scientists apply Latin
best. For instance, a dying star's
final breath is a *nebula*.
But my favorite is *ex*, meaning "lacking"
or "out of." Examples: *to extirpate*,
to exsanguinate. A cell dividing
will arrange its chromosomes
into a line of *ex*es, a heap
of cells, waiting.

*

On the day when I lay, feet in stirrups, possibly grateful
for unconsciousness while the doctor scraped and sucked,
what did my mind turn to? I had no dreams.

The embryo neither; it lacked half
its parts. When I awoke, my heart was still
beating too quickly.

*

Mrs. Roentgen, tell me what future you saw
when you first laid eyes on that X-ray—
your black bones, your incandescent flesh.

Common Disaster No. 1

A few months before she died, my grandmother
whispered that she wouldn't
leave him: her husband was doing his best.
No, she shook her head.

That was a week before my husband and I
found her half dressed, when my step-
grandfather shrugged: *Urine dries fast.*
And I shouldn't have been surprised
when he struck like a hammer
into gunpowder—*Don't you fucking*
touch her! This isn't your fucking house!
I remember the whites of my husband's eyes
as he turned the wheelchair, as I tried to grab
still-full pill bottles and underpants—

We brought her home.
And she lived a little while.

Days are short. The mosquitoes are out,
hovering among the tulip trees. My husband
turns steaks over charcoal, and I tell him
about my last patient of the day: a hard-
living man who'd said, *I'd rather die*
than let you take my leg. My grandmother's
mail still arrives: *Enjoy the credit*
you deserve! Buy two get one free!
Rib eyes smoke on our plates.
Someone's dog won't stop barking.

Notes in a Minor Key

My best friend said the only way she'd find God
is if she got locked up in prison, & she'd pick
Jesus over the rest because he has the most
subscribers. I mean, a couple days ago when

I learned that birds can vocalize two separate
notes at the same time & that there are islands
inhabited by ancient reptiles simultaneously
nearly extinct yet powerful enough to kill

prey in seconds—I, too, almost
believed. But it's easy for things to slide
back. This week's employee newsletter
includes this acknowledgment: *O Lord, so many*

souls in a hot truck. O they burned up, & we
cringe at imagining it. Were you there
with them? Please, Lord, say that you were.
I try to imagine how it's possible to hover

& still be God. Maybe it's like asking why
music in a minor key feels more profound, & is it
just the way human brains were made?
What about birds, what sounds

saddest to them? Naturalists say form
follows function. Clever hands & avian throats—
in a garden of earthly delights, is grief
our function? Any other two-legged beasts

could sing, unnoticed, inside our grottoes
of fire. How do our small-tailed lives
fit themselves to the locks
through which God threads his fingers?

Aubade with Chicxulub Crater and Extinction

When the world immediately fractured
down the asteroid's shock impact, spring

had already warmed the shallows half
a continent away, the sturgeon rolling

through slow rivers, locked in ancient
ritual. Here, meat-eating

dinosaurs tracked along shorelines,
their feathers scattered over mud

yellow with pollen.
These are scientific facts.

What we don't know is the hour
our asteroid arrived that day. Artists' renditions

depict animals with faces tilted up
at a second sun, or else monstrous

tides, ash blotting the sky. Preoccupied
with our own future, we find ourselves unable

to understand an earth that didn't belong to us,
our minds dismissing the difference

between unluckiness and atomic megatons
as easily as radiation streams though flesh.

Still, the thought hovers, like the infinite
instant of impact. Like a star incinerating into dawn.

Charles Darwin to His Wife, Emma, 1851

after Jenna Le

I've spent too much time thinking

it is interesting to contemplate an entangled bank

about inheritance how the well-fed house cat who

clothed with many plants of many kinds

has never been taught can leap high

with birds singing on the bushes

to swat a sparrow from mid-flight

with various insects flitting about and with worms

or why without thought she delivers the killing

crawling through the damp earth and to reflect

yet also lifts her blind kitten in a velvet grip

that these elaborately constructed forms so different

it must be some kind of instinct to love

from each other and dependent on each other

our children so dearly that when a child grows

in so complex a manner have all been produced

sick and knows she is dying we need no lessons

by laws acting around us

to cling to each small wretched lie

Two-Headed Dog

> Moscow is a huge city where hundreds of people die daily from various causes. . . . We shall take what we need from the dead in order to save the living.
>
> —DR. VLADIMIR DEMIKHOV, father of transplant surgery, 1959

1

Brodyaga means "tramp,"
meaning this big young bitch
was plucked from the streets. *Shavka*—
"mongrel"—is self-explanatory.

2

The doctor clarifies how lucky
they are: *Two heads are better*
than one. Small bright Shavka lolls

her tongue, jumps and smiles. Brodyaga's
already sedated—hard to picture her wolflike
form roaming the streets.
The surgery itself takes less

than two hours. Anesthetize, shave.
Open the larger dog's nape, cut through
to the spine. Ensure the host wound

is large. Now the graft: open the little dog's
chest and neck. Dissect down. Vessel
by vessel, isolate the heart
from its head, and, with each suture, join

that head to the vast, waiting wound.
To free the graft, slice away the rest
of Shavka.

3

Now, what can the heads do?
The doctor shows each one blinking
and—when the narcosis has worn off—
eating, lapping water.

The graft head has no stomach;
what it drinks spills from a tube
onto the floor.

4

After surgery, instruments are sterilized,
the furnace turned on. The amputated body
of what was this morning a barking dog
drifts into the sky.

In the yard, the host finally stands,
gold-black tail shivering, clamped tight.

The heads tremble.

The Amount of Death and Pain in the City Was Extraordinary

—RICHARD WEIR of Human Rights Watch,
The Washington Post, April 21, 2022

It's been reported: In Bucha,
people are collecting bodies stuffed
with bullets, hands tied behind their backs.
Today, a father arrives,
recognizes the shape of his son's soles, the long
toes. He ties a tag to the mud-
stained ankle; they won't lose him
again. Imagine those gray feet—
thirty-some years old—sticking out beneath
the corner of a flowered bedsheet
spread over a patch of dirt, the father
folding it back, fist to mouth—

People Are Sad

> . . . but what can we do? Nothing. Just cry.
>
> —BILAL GAF, a Kurdish refugee speaking to the BBC
> on the drowning of Artin Iran-Nejad, June 2021

today I see Jesus in my toast yet another sighting / his face

a little burnt / his mouth frowning

this is the headline on the BBC / *Body of Baby Who Died in Channel Found*

in Norway / on my commute I think about the crossing

lurch of the dinghy eight-foot waves / how people insisted

God walked on water

when I was a kid I watched spindly insects skitter across ponds / they did

whatever they pleased / they irritated me

with brainless confidence their monopoly

on miracles / I'd throw stones

just to see them sink

a supreme court opinion June 24, 2022

after Joan Naviyuk Kane

GOD BLESS AMERICA
GO~~D BLESS~~ AMERICA
GOD ~~BLES~~S AMERICA
~~GOD B~~LESS AMERICA
~~GOD BLES~~S AME~~RICA~~
~~GOD BLESS~~ AMERICA
~~G~~O~~D BLESS~~ AMERICA
~~G~~O~~D BLESS AMERICA~~
GOD ~~BLESS AMERICA~~

samuel alito: saying
or implying
that the court is becoming
an illegitimate
institution or
questioning
our integrity crosses
~~an important~~
~~line~~

Ghazal

On TV, astronauts land in Kazakhstan. Behind them, god,
the locusts—a welcoming party—proclaim no fear of God.

Folks came of age, once, under Chernobyl's stars.
That was when a sabbatical was easier for God.

Back then, crowds came and went. Unless a giantess
or wolf-boy stepped onstage, hardly anyone became God.

Today, my cousin pretends she's not coughing blood, that she's losing
weight on purpose. I ask myself, how can I take it up with God?

A young surgeon hid his diagnosis. People whispered, like flies: *Why*
didn't he tell anyone—see a doctor, get some help, my God—

There's the writing on the wall: Our universe is built like a bomb.
Surely no one still thinks God is listening, let alone God.

Fast-forward again. A man steps in front of some tanks.
I cry, wondering whether God will ever be that kind of God.

You see, I, too, hear angels in my head. But will God
cast them out—another miracle just for the sake of God?

The Last Surgeon in Mariupol

Dear devil, I wish you'd tell me
how this solar eclipse burns
across my retinas, and why neoplasia
returns home to the walls

of bodies and brains. Was it for the same
reason that you took Rimbaud's poetry,
then his life? I think surely
you must've wept all the way from Aden to—

Let me cast a little magic, open
your skull, take out the shrapnel.
Your dura will still shatter, but it shouldn't
define who we are. What things matter

to you? Today, I stitched
two seams in the dark, pulled the edges
over the face. And were you there, listening
as the knocks under the rubble slowed and slowed?

We Would Welcome a Full Investigation into This Matter

—MARK MILLER, US State Department, on asking Israel to investigate the killing of six-year-old Hind Rajab and paramedics Yousef Zeino and Ahmed al-Madhoun, *The Washington Post,* April 16, 2024

It's been reported: the exact

location of a small girl trapped
with her family, the precise trajectory

of the ambulance sent
to save her. She is on the line—

please come get me please—

she is only two miles away. Her family,
bodies in the car.

Imagine, then, how to
say to a child:
if we are cut off

if it gets dark or the phone's
batteries run out can you remember
something for me dear

we are coming we won't
stop until we find you

rest now you can
close your eyes let's pretend to make
the tanks invisible—

Imagine how long before you stop.

Bosworth Field

Centuries of winter plowing
and continuous progress have leveled
the ground—no casual observer now would
think about how much iron our ancestors laid down.
Iron, having lives of its own, moves cyclically
in and out of bodies, like rain. It's true, if you combed
the land, you'd find old Roman
coins, Tudor hat pins—just things
people lost. But iron returns to the earth invisibly—
nobody abandons steel to the aftermath
of crows and foxes slinking afield, counting
the dead. No, blood seeps through the soil
until it's swallowed. It's like breathing, almost,
how we've forgotten that this rusted marsh still
exists everywhere—an endless ice-limned
surface, ripening its crop of faces.

Concerning a Crushed Temple

Case XXII from the Edwin Smith Papyrus, a surgical treatise c. ~1700 BCE

The ancient word for "crush"
can be translated as *split* or *shatter*,

even *perforate. Puncture.* In this case,
any variation still means a grave

wound inflicted on the side of a skull.
The author states that if a person suffers

from a crushed temple, the nostrils and ears
will discharge their blood. The person becomes

speechless. When archaeologists unearthed
Younger Lady's mummy in the tomb of Amenhotep II,

everyone thought she was a royal woman, possibly
a king's daughter. She must have been beautiful,

people said, except, of course, she's been dead
over three millennia and half her head's

destroyed. In photos, it's obvious
that you could, if you wanted to, look through

her gashed-open face straight
into the rupture of her brain. And if,

as scholars say, her terrible injury happened
before death, there remain no words

to describe the unmistakable sound
of impact, when a body follows its head

to the ground. In her halo of blood,
who knows whether she had time to beg?

This might be why, before poetry
came of age, people carved

animal-faced gods
into granite: shadows

of men and women perfected
by centuries of grief, fierce

lion- and hawk-headed bodies to carry
all we cannot speak.

II

The *Yijing*: a pandemic apocrypha

the headlines don't seem
to agree with one another which according to some
observers is reassuring and means none of it can really be
that bad

65. Verge
Waiting in blood, you place your feet before the precipice, though you do not know whether the rain that fills your body is correct, nor the clouds that adorn your feet. Has the rain run clearly? Waiting in blood means listening for what travels; below, three white wolves look up. Are they worthwhile if you go in opposite directions?

the weather keeps
changing
strange how the weatherman always reminds
everyone to turn off the tap
while brushing their teeth

66. Fire Walking
Days rotate. If you are blind to spruce cracking among the flames, you are not peaceful. Clouds should not follow.

Christmas makes its appearance late
the supply chain they say but soon we'll get back
the price of chicken
is just too high

67. Same Tears
A bull profits with its horns. Just as when the wind bodes, townspeople bite noses and feet. Biting off noses and feet means having gone into a dark valley where arrows are lost. Weeping and lamenting.

the papers are making much
of the CDC's statement
in a crisis

what do we do with those doctors and nurses

is it seven days or five or zero

nobody has really defined
a *crisis*

subzero this week's forecast
risk of flu plane
crash shark attack gold
standard comparisons all
we lack

82. Hesitation
To drag ancient trees is regretful. If cities collapse, what is gained by dragging? Coming and going, thunder repeats for a thousand miles.

hospital press statement
in accordance with exceedingly difficult
decisions limited
resources we must identify the most

likely to survive

98. Split Marrow
Horses sleep on the shore. Do you continue to the end? Sleeping, you suddenly hear a voice. An old history.

a warzone
like walking

into a war
zone

100. Vastness

Lightning is still difficult. The jar cracked; it cannot be put back. You weep tears of blood, for what lasts?

Afternoon Rounds

The sun slants
through the windows of the skybridge.
Outside, the hospital's rooftop is flat, seamed
with steel. I see the white cross
on the helipad, and the turkey buzzard
sunning himself against the glass
in his usual spot. When he turns toward me,
the skin of his neck crumples into wet tissue.
Three stories down, a family—almost
miniature—waves at the helicopter
tilting away. They don't know about
the child whose skull floods with blood,
or the woman whose aorta has split
like sausage. That the helicopter isn't
coming back is the secret I don't want
to hold. When the buzzard raises
his wings, serrated shadows
slide under the windows.

Forms of Water

A friend tells me if I were desperate enough, I wouldn't settle
for *any of this*—wave of the hand. Perhaps she means
the middle-aged sagging of my core, where I once believed
I needed to sweat. Or maybe that I ought to act
more grateful. That I don't have, for example, cancer,
and can do whatever people
without cancer do.

Reading the headlines to my daughters: Siberia has melted,
and a graveyard of long-dead reindeer is spewing anthrax.
Havana Syndrome isn't new; during the Cold War,
Operation Hello used microwaves to make people think
they were hearing voices. *How can you hear*
something that doesn't exist?

I take my mom to her appointment. We forget
her glucometer, and the doctor reminds us
about diet and exercise. I take myself
to the grocery store—black plums are in season.
Dad and the girls like them. They take the stones
and hope for seedlings. But I feel cold

remembering January, when the ditches sank
under the weight of rain, and people
sank under the weight of their lungs. I cannot
forget my grandmother's eyes in the monochrome
photos, when she was still a medical student and didn't know
that in seventy years, in the bed she'd never
leave again, she'd ask me
when she could go.

Trees on our street haven't recovered
from the freeze. Most people
aren't masking anymore. When I see familiar
faces, strangers speak their words.

Common Disaster No. 2

1

Today another patient
chokes: *Don't*
let me die—

When her heart says *No,* there is so much
noise in the room—so many people
swarming, and then things
inserted—

Her legs jerk with every compression.

It's 11:46 when we call it.
Over the phone, I listen
to her husband's sobs.

2

When I walk out of the hospital,
the moon warps the asphalt, drags
itself along each parked car.

3

Sometimes after work I get sloppy: I'll use
teabags instead of loose-leaf, eat
bread straight from the bag. But I never
forget to open the fridge and check
each item, pretending this is all I need.

4

I do not cry.

5

Time of death:
Time of death:
Time of death:

6

There's a crow that likes to sit on the streetlamp right outside the hospital's entrance. He is sleek, indifferent. A few months ago, I would have wanted to kill him.

X-Ray

This spring, I got sick—
a cough I picked up at the hospital
that got so bad I thought

I would die. For weeks
after, I felt I'd never
return to normal.

In my bed—short of breath
out of it—I became an expert
at finding weird phenomena

to pore over. Such as: How few people
dare return to Chernobyl's zone
of alienation—yes, it's called that—

yet wolves living there are healthier
than ever. In fact, they never
left, multiplying now,

congregating in the most
radioactive places.
Every day, I added to my list—

diamond rains on Neptune,
people who ate arsenic to get high.
If others could imagine making a nuclear

forest home, or picture the ecstasy
in poison, why hadn't I thought to imagine
the fear of a person reduced

to one desperate plea for air,
when, despite breathing
faster than a panicked horse, the body

still suffocates? These days,
I think about the way my X-ray
looked, the unremarkable

whiteout wedge I'd seen
many times before, when it had (always)
belonged to someone else,

when I'd quizzed the med students
during rounds, tested their ability
to make the diagnosis, then pronounced:

Here's your garden-variety
example. Memorize it. It's a classic
you'll see your whole life.

The Shores of Babylon

2022 CE

When everything started, the newscasters said
all would be back to normal sooner
than later. Now, heat uncoils
itself outside the caves where people
cut their days beneath Jupiter's vapid twirl.
Fallout dried up.

*

There is always
a *prior to.* For instance, the last
of any species is an *endling,*
or else a *terminarch,* who strains
to remember—or forget—another's body
leaning in. I remind myself
that scientists once studied the bones
of mammoths in cliff shadows, while everyone else
decided that we didn't
drive the beasts over the edge.
They went on their own.

*

I am tired. I walk among
the half-buried, my handprints pressed
into the sky; the emptied houses
semaphore endlessly. All the sediment
we called God's *bad rains*—who could say
what now drags its tail through?
There are some who will survive
any spectacle. I hold
a mirror to my lips to see
what happens.

Ghazal

Sunk into our planet's center, a lead weight spins into nowhere.
Human minds simmer like diesel, ready to explode out of nowhere.

I love breathing heat from open flames. I can't take being shut
up or forced underground, as if vultures didn't swarm everywhere.

Also, it was a lie: Anaximander thinking the sun was a wheel of fire.
His math actually showed the sun's the patron saint of nowhere.

In Rome, wasps shone under cornices like jewels—Cleopatra's stung
but never died. Imagine her as the Emperor of anywhere.

Sometimes, at night, I wake, as if hearing smashed fountains
brim over in Al-Andalus. Where are those gardens now, if not nowhere?

Who, as a matter of fact, is allowed to return to the forests, to their
ancient homelands? Even trees are absent in the middle-of-nowhere.

As usual, my protests rise past ozone to the clutter of low orbit.
Meltwater always runs bright, stings, then disappears nowhere.

Kalends

It's been a year since the air
retreated and everything arrived late—
winter, the rain. Breath.

A friend says to me, *Everyone is afraid*
of dying now. I remember my grandmother waiting
to die. When she opened her mouth
at the end, the sounds were already gone.

Across the city, newborn mountains
push into the sky. When I leave the hospital at the end
of my shift, glaciers over the peaks
glitter like minor galaxies.

Time & Again

For the sake of the present / let's just admit that thigh-deep mud & poison gas & running into machine-gun fire / still belong to us all the glass-eyed / survivors who said sundown was almost worse than morning slaughters / night when stretcher-bearers could finally reach the duckboards / run toward the day's groans caught / on barbed wire / surgeons waited in casualty clearing with their indelible ink two / possibilities / *attempt* & *no hope* by midnight under the flare of kerosene they would've plowed through how many limbs entrails & skulls at least a hundred per surgeon per night / months / years / in no way do I compare this to a pandemic but maybe / nature of human memory the definition / of nature how many *don't believe the lies* & destinations / you never return from / who gets the ventilator what becomes of those making decisions it's almost / the opposite of a siege inside the hospital walls / the gasping / is it shock / we had to tie down people's hands to stop them pulling out the breathing tubes air had / a taste what happens / on a front so far away / I think those in charge call it *wastage*

I Dream of Animals During the Pandemic

I find a lobster in the swimming
pool. It looks me in the eye, the way
people do when they don't
want to, and with a voice like glass says,
Your grandmother
is dying again.

I've read that some animals in the wild
can live for hundreds of years, but I wake up
before I can say, *I'm sorry I'm sorry*
I am the doctor who couldn't
save you. What does it matter—
"visitors" still aren't allowed
in nursing homes, unless someone is
dying and they have to be
really dying. Not slowly,
not day after day, in the small quiet
bed, but the way a fleet creature
dies, the crack of its leg
shattering the pale air.

So, I write junk
all day, a sleep-drunk
welter I swerve to avoid,
like a line of nighttime
elk strung out on the road,
a flash of green-lit
eyes, dark rumps and rising,
falling breath, vaporous, yet
almost solid against the grain
of my headlights the instant
before we collide.

Seeing My Patient's CT Scan

1

I can't help thinking for the thousandth
time: Isn't it strange that *man* in Irish
is spelled *fear*? And pronounced like *far*?

2

The hospital's cream-colored walls
have begun falling in—a familiar
anxious routine. The 33-year-old
father of three sits in his room
on the sixth floor, liver crowded
with masses. His youngest climbs
onto his lap as I let him know we're still waiting
for the biopsy results. When I walk to my car,
it's spring, almost summer. The cicadas are
out, climbing the same trees
their parents did.

3

In school, they taught us
to give a "warning shot"
before delivering bad news:
I'm sorry, I have
bad news.
Suddenly I have too many
words, and not enough.

4

The father turns his head, struggles
not to cry. A flight of starlings pivots
at eye level outside his high
window, then moves higher
out of sight. His daughter bursts
back in, shouting, *Daddy, Daddy, why
are ants so small?*

After the Diagnosis

December rain floods
the churned mud, melts fields
parched by frost. Crows gather
like seed among the junipers.
These things I can still say.
But how to stitch together
the day, when my grip on any hour
slips beneath the riverbed? How to
loosen the margins of flesh
hardening into stone the shape
of flesh? Everywhere the trees
grow, greener than ever.

Diorama

Standing on Wilshire Boulevard, I can't get enough
of the asphalt's stench, the archaic drama:

tusked fiberglass mammoth forever
dying, sinking into the black lake, panicked

mate and infant stuck on the shore with
the cars and construction-zone apartments.

In 1967, Howard Bell loaded the male onto
a trailer in front of his studio and towed it

to La Brea with his Volkswagen. Today,
the female's body sways on barely

visible moorings. Orange cones dot
the park, warning against new tar seeps.

I find a stick, poke the sludge emerging
between grass blades, and immediately it grips,

pulls me close. I can't tug the stick
free. Fresh tar clings to my fingers—first time

in 200 million years this once-living stuff
surfaces, escaping the afterlife.

A newspaper critic once said this tableau
is outdated "kitsch." The morning

air smells like shit. Before me, a horse-size
child on the edge, unmovable, almost

certain to plunge in.

Ghazal

Silks traveled through many hands, starting in the Orient.
Don't tell me, love, God made the stars for us to orient.

Before we ever started, war gathered across continents.
Still, love, I'd forgotten your penchant to disorient.

Your ash rains again from the west, blotting the lords of the sky.
Tell me how to set fire to pearls—that blinding orient.

You return to the argument: *Let me show you how to . . .*
—always said I was too unsophisticated to orient.

Oolong uncoils in my cup, your sugar on my tongue.
Who thought I'd turn infidel? Your sense of orientation?

I can't pay your price anymore—my useless milk, wasted blood.
Only your skill to distract. It's ornamental, almost oriental.

The moon covers the sun. It's God, not astronomy, remember?
Never mind where I've gone—the sky's too overcast to reorient.

Summer Palace

When glaciers retreated from the plains, most animals followed them into the sky. Only the saiga—antelopes tricked by cold-weather feints—stayed. Now, they circle in their last great migration. The ghost of Genghis Khan tells me these things calmly, the same way he says that meltwater is fresh, not salt, and at least 1 in 200 men today descends from his own body. I know it's true, science has proved it. I say to him, so, it's possible you really are my ancestor. Look how I ride, and fast. I'm certain to learn to shoot from a gallop. I know this because memories from those alive in 1949 are as far back as my genealogy goes. That was when thin papers burned on their spines, flew like sparks into the sky. At gunpoint, on threat of family, they made my grandmother's sister eat bowlfuls of hair and sleep with the dead in their open graves. To this day, my parents like to tell me it can happen again. Run first, think later. Be ready. At this, the Khan seems to regard my story with pity. Hair and dead bodies, he muses. In the summer country, we'd have cooked your wish into a diet of antelope flesh, or perhaps small arrowheads pressed into your back. Don't imagine for a second I will tell you what to call yourself—you know how careless people are with names. In the act of remembering: bones all sound the same.

Sand-People of Sutton Hoo

Adjacent to the royal barrows,
archaeologists find another burial ground.
Each grave opened is a squared-off pit
where the dead seem idle,
or interrupted. For instance,
that one, his skull—separate
from his neck—grins
between his knees. Here, a woman
appears the way I might look
if I lay down quietly
and died. If a warm hand
then pressed closed my eyes
and wiped everything else away.
To be forgiven.
I lean in for a closer inspection.
No, her head is also unlatched,
carefully turned
face down, facing hell.

Islandic

with lines from Derek Mahon and Henrik Ibsen

All this time: as if rivers
survive on anything
but water.

When I was seven, I poured salt
over a clutch of snails. Have you ever
broken a thermometer? Watched

the mercury squirm? Surely,
it's a kind of human activity.
On Socotra, poets sang until they flew

up skirts of trees. I've read that some say
Eden once was an island,
but never mind Bikini.

There! *A door bangs*
with diminished confidence.
Who's worse than red tides? Anyone

listening? I find the shore
of Manchu's poems; they are extinct
in the wild. Geckos lick their eyes

because it's better than air.
I once believed a horoscope, one
red star, could tell me

how to survive this life.
What's that line?—*Below,*
sound of a door slamming shut.

Continents scarred with cuneiform.
Look! The carapace splits
when detached.

Common Disaster No. 3

At parties, people joke about spitting
into tubes, then being told what percentage of them
is Neanderthal. I am more or less

the same—worried about my inability
to make small talk, air pollution,
and guns, or, when falling asleep, failing to make

a diagnosis. Growing up in Oklahoma,
I knew the drill
when tornado sirens went off: Stay away from

windows and mirrors, hide in a windowless
room, crouch down hands-on-head
in the center of school.

For other kids, earthquakes. Hurricanes.
In reality, we all endure our personal
disasters. In medical school, we learned that

early radiologists believed the erythema dose
was safe. I once felt the need to keep
a small radio under my Care Bears pillow,

maybe already afraid of a sub-
lethal hit. Our professor said even an apocalyptic
exposure just turns the skin pink, at first.

Death itself takes a week
to occur. We students
wrote it down. Later, I was surprised

to read that other, now-extinct human
species, too, had big brains, crossed
oceans. Perhaps they were the first

scientists to analyze our world—
vectors of bird flight, omens
composed of entrails—brave individuals

with no aversion to recklessness.
Still, the grackle's whoop
sets me off—an unwinding alarm

so familiar. Electric. In the Pleistocene
I think the air was colder.
Elephants once grew fur.

Ensenada

In December, we drive south to visit friends.
It's empty at the beach—high tide—but

the next morning, an object like a huge
mound of sand has appeared on the shore, as if

shoved up by the waves. When we approach,
it resolves into patchy fur, a swollen,

sunburnt face. The wind blows away from us.
Wikipedia says only the walrus and elephant seal

are bigger, but that's obviously a lie.
None of us has ever seen a thing this enormous

in decay. Unsure what else to do,
we shoo away the gulls. The sea lion bull's

remaining eye gapes silently at us.
As we debate who to call,

men in public works vests arrive.
They dig, then disappear

into the hole. Sand leaps out on its own.
It is Christmas. The town is quiet.

We cross the boardwalk under a sheet
of clouds, looking to outrun the rain.

The Blue House: a Feng Shui Portrait

after Jose Hernandez Diaz

The blue house sits at the end of a T-intersection. The blue house has a front door leading to a staircase. The blue house has a pantry full of ghosts. The ghosts could fly in a line from the front door up the stairs and through the attic, but they don't. The blue house's fiber-optic is the fastest on the street. The blue house is bluer than van Gogh's painting. The blue house is always priced more than you can afford. The blue house's address begins with a four. When it rains, the blue house's runoff tends blue. Sinks tighten around their drains. The blue house grows predictable in winter. The blue house once had a chimney. The blue house would rather not talk anymore. The blue house, shivering under its roof.

I Wonder as I Listen to Beethoven's Symphony No. 9

if the voices I hear weren't
already some form of prayer / would I
like Napoleon's troops dying
in the Russian winter / use my hands
that have never held a gun / only scalpel
to slit open a mare's
belly / climb inside the steaming red
cave of her ribs / and live
in that silence / unborn animal-
child / is it possible
those now-dead men thought
of naked Atlantic tides flinching
from a shore I also know / it's no coincidence
that *pray* is pronounced *prey* / as in
have you seen or heard things that aren't
really there / it's a standard question
what shall I say / when every night
I wait for the mares' return / their bodies
rustle like feathers / they arrive
crushing sugar in their mouths
sonic / more than blindingly
bright

Grotto

I like how fire-eating bats drip and grow
their rivalries at dusk—furred membranes,
furrowed wing bones.

When they descend through eaves
of stone, they rise again
in inflorescence. I reach for the first

fist. Flint. It feels light,
like pigment or flame,
as if enough to shape anything

I desire. Which is the story
of a girl we know:
girl with no champion, sent out

hooded in red, or dressed
as sacrifice for greater
good. Surrendered to wilderness, girl

who, when almost dead, discovers
a house standing
on its single clawed leg.

Long ago alive, the house
sighs, spreads its feathers
over her shoulders to wait.

Girl, who finds courage
to whisper to the gathering beasts—
Fire-eaters. Feast. Girl,

who recognizes
her own kind, her eyes becoming
brilliant like theirs.

Now she slithers
under leaf litter, stalks
the canopy—long ringed tail

swaying silently.
She sleeps underwater.
Who hasn't wanted

to be that girl: prism of sharp
white fangs, flurry
of absence and air?

After My Daughters Tell Me They Are Learning How to Identify Animals at School

We arrive late to the zoo—most of the inhabitants
are drowsy, heads tucked under wings and tails.
I buy each girl a popcorn and a slushy, and we head over
to the big cats. The lions take us in, then close
their eyes. Their outlines are as familiar as children's
book illustrations. *Can we go to the gift shop now?*
my girls ask. But I insist we see
a few more. The next exhibit seems empty
at first. Then a curious dark
shape emerges from the shade, a massive
stiff mane standing along its spine.
The boy next to us says, *It doesn't even look*
like a proper elephant.

The animal fixes its eyes on us, its heavy pelt
twitching. Unexpectedly, its mouth opens in a high-
pitched call, as if drawing upon something hidden—

the sound strips the air of all words.
Mountains rise before us.

For a moment, my girls squeeze their eyes shut. *Now*
can we go?

I look over my shoulder—the creature
turns. Grass closes behind it.
A humid reprieve drifts beneath the sun.

Sightseeing

It was 3 p.m., our last day in Iceland, and sunset
was nine hours away. We parked along the highway, listening
to the car's tick, the wind muttering over the lava field.

Through the scoria we walked—until finally, half disbelieving,
we arrived at the head of a track beside a low stone wall.
It was as if I could see the Vikings of mythology,

Halli and Leiknir, their thick-boned hands again clearing the path,
hefting moss-riddled boulders. You nodded: *Yes, I see it.*
Their graves lay beyond the wall, marked only

by a cairn. What were we after, you and I, the heirs of refugees?
We were newly married, longing to trace the shape
of our descent from people—family—whose strange hand-painted

records we neither knew existed nor could read. Yet here,
ancestors were everywhere, common as fitted stones
or midnight dusk. Stories stacked upon earth.

How we looked away, two foreigners in the wilderness, turning
and turning to the ash plumes rising from the turf.

Dream of the Astrobleme

Though no map of Iceland records a meteorite
impact, I still remember the turn off the road,
the black crater walls like a silent
mouth rising above the fields.

But this must have been before
our daughters, before realizing we shouldn't
run into the center of the remains of 1.8 million
Hiroshimas scorched into diamonds. And then you
asked, *Where is the other—the second crater?*
because you'd read that some asteroids
are twinned, yoked together for billions
of years as they hurtle through emptiness.

We agreed: *We are no longer*
two, but one flesh. In that moment we were
two stars that to the very end
would never escape one another's
gravity, our own bright collision.

Incarnation

after Mag Gabbert

Because in another universe, I was once the red star Betelgeuse.

Because decades later, I am being married off.

Because horses went extinct in the New World, but conquistadors brought them back—I have seen them.

Because girls are smaller than boys, girls must be more responsible.

Because the great Marat was killed in his bathtub by a girl.

Because after her execution, the examiners were disappointed she was a virgin.

Because isn't that the most important fact.

Because the white ash of Vesuvius protected the bodies it burned.

And sweet liquid pressed from grapes is worth more than grapes.

Because I must bleed every month.

Because God created and said it was good.

Because even dogs only rut twice a year.

Because I try to remember that in Thebes and Babylon, the goddesses of love were also the goddesses of war, and they went into battle with ten thousand faces.

Because he always blames me for the chase.

Because in this universe, I'm still running.

Kite

We escape the city, drive
to where Gulf meets sand.
At the waterline, our daughters

set up camp with plastic pails
and shovels, and we unfold chairs
into the surf, read *National Geographic*

and Stephen King paperbacks.
The girls take out their squid-shaped
kite and toss it into the wind.

Rainbow ribbons flare.
Flocks of pelicans bank away.
This is how we attempt our absurd

apology: for the city, the heat,
for what emerges from the day-
to-day—that we understood

the raging world, and still we
created. The girls run with the kite
streaming ahead. They stretch their arms

to one another, laughing as if
in a secret story. As if in a haze
of joy, the kite might begin to rise

past gulls and clouds, comet-tail
snapping, steadily pulling
children, who look back and wave.

Ghazal

This time out, I return as a mountain lion. I don't mean to survive: exile
crossing highways, caught on camera traps. But I find no other exit—

I don't believe in God or reincarnation, not when my body still
outlives my memories. As if a body isn't a form of exile.

To speak one's native language as a foreigner. I move the silences
around—blue-green mountains draped in rain I'll never see in exile.

Every thousand years, the meadow floods. What's left behind:
a film of minnows sparkling and twisting in the grass. Exquisite exiles.

In dreams, I reel from loss to loss. Each ghost I encounter recites
my greatest fears. As if I were the only stranger speaking from exile.

Hollywood—bright letters at night. The lone male stalks downhill. Eye-
shine, long feline sweep. He does not swerve, my veteran of exile.

On the ridge where once I spotted deer, I find candy wrappers, old flyers.
I hold my breath as long as it takes. The things you do in exile.

Still Life

The backyard foxes are lean
this winter, and the birds bright.
Most days I can't bring myself
to do anything but watch the vixen
root for something. A run of good
days means I'll spend hours rearranging
the pantry, as if preparing to paint
a Dutch still life. All that's missing
is a milkmaid. Or a dead bird. My dress,
wrinkled and sleeveless, is nothing
like the sky. The foxes grow
thinner, and I wonder
whether I should feed them, though
I don't really know what they eat.
Nights stretch and I sleep
little, but it's the days, the sun
at four o'clock, that are the most
difficult—when the movement
of clouds appears full
of peril. People once drilled holes
into other people's skulls, just to let
that darkness out.

ACKNOWLEDGMENTS

Grateful acknowledgment to the editors of the following publications in which these poems first appeared, sometimes in earlier versions or under different titles:

Allium, A Journal of Poetry and Prose: "Dream of the Astrobleme" and "The Blue House: a Feng Shui Portrait"
Bacopa Literary Review: "Sightseeing"
Bicoastal Review: "Sand-People of Sutton Hoo"
Bracken: "Kalends"
CALYX Journal: "Common Disaster No. 2"
Crab Creek Review: "After My Daughters Tell Me They Are Learning How to Identify Animals at School"
Dialogist: "People Are Sad"
Diode Poetry Journal: "Boreal Time" and "Ghazal [This time out, I return as a mountain lion . . .]"
Figure 1: "Common Disaster No. 1"
The Florida Review: "Aubade with Chicxulub Crater and Extinction"
Four Way Review: "Ghazal [Silks traveled through many hands . . .]"
Gulf Coast: "Islandic"
Hayden's Ferry Review: "The *Yijing*: a pandemic apocrypha"
Honey Literary: "I Wonder as I Listen to Beethoven's Symphony No. 9" and "Notes in a Minor Key"
Huizache: "Grotto" and "Ghazal [Down the hole now . . .]"
Jet Fuel Review: "Summer Palace"
The Journal of the American Medical Association: "I Dream of Animals During the Pandemic"
Los Angeles Review: "Ghazal [On TV, astronauts land in Kazakhstan . . .]"
The Massachusetts Review: "a supreme court opinion 24 June 2022" and "The Amount of Death and Pain in the City Was Extraordinary"

ONLY POEMS: "Ghazal [Sunk into our planet's center . . .]"
Palette Poetry: "Concerning a Crushed Temple"
Pleiades: "Bosworth Field"
Puerto del Sol: "Seeing My Patient's CT Scan" and "After the Diagnosis"
RHINO: "Still Life"
Sixth Finch: "Diorama" and "Kite"
Southern Humanities Review: "The Last Surgeon in Mariupol"
Sugar House Review: "Afternoon Rounds"
SWWIM Every Day: "I Have Seen My Death"
The Shore: "Forms of Water"
Tupelo Quarterly: "The Shores of Babylon"
Under a Warm Green Linden: "Incarnation"
Water~Stone Review: "X-Ray"

I owe debts of gratitude to many people. To my parents, Shiufei and Peter, who nurtured me since the beginning, then let me find my own path. To my brother, Kelvin, and Joy, Wen, Di, and Rocky, fellow travelers in adventure, with many more to come. To my grandmother Shu-Fang, physician par excellence, who loved me the way no one else could. To my grandparents, aunts, uncles, and cousins, for helping shape who I am today, and to the Le family, for welcoming me as a daughter. Thank you to Chelsea B. DesAutels and Mag Gabbert, my first teachers, without whom there would be no poems. Thank you to Lisa Ampleman and Nicola Mason, who believed in this book and guided it into the world. To the entire Acre Books team, for all you do.

To the friends who have cheered me on, including Syshan Doun; Jennifer Han and Maggie Ham and Andrea Oh; Jose Hernandez Diaz; Elana Hoffman; Jan and Ceri Jones; Reshma Lakhiani and Robert Liou; Maria Nguyen; Van Phan and Nikhil Lobo; Rae Rozman; Asmaa Safadi and Kuytaba Alsafadi; Lisa and Jeffrey Stanton; and Travis Vandergriff and Rodrigo Zepeda.

Thank you to Joan Naviyuk Kane for her generosity and unending enthusiasm for my work and to Amit Majmudar and Kevin Prufer for lending their beautiful, kind words. Thanks also to Claire Wahmanholm and the Poetry Society of America for selecting my work for the Robert H. Winner Memorial Award, and to his family and friends for honoring me in his memory. My thanks to

Allison Hedge Coke, Sergio Lima, and Leonora Simonovis, for selecting and supporting me as an Idyllwild Arts Writers Week fellow, and to Paul Gross and Jenna Le, for bringing me onto the editorial team at *Pulse—voices from the heart of medicine.* I am grateful to have worked with Neal Barshes, David Short, the DeBakey Medical Foundation, and Baylor College of Medicine on the Michael E. DeBakey Medical Student Poetry Award.

To everyone who has chosen to spend time with my poems: you honor me with your fellowship.

To my physician colleagues around the world, for your sacrifices.

And to Eleanor, Eva, and Danny, my greatest love.